SECRETS OF THE RAINFOREST

PREDATORS AND PREY

BY MICHAEL CHINERY

CHERRYTREE BOOKS

A Cherrytree Book

Designed and produced by
A S Publishing

First published 2000
by Cherrytree Press
327 High Street
Slough
Berkshire
SL1 1TX

British Library Cataloguing in Publication Data

Chinery, Michael
Predators and prey. — (Secrets of the rainforest)
1.Rain forest animals — Juvenile literature
2.Predatory animals — Juvenile literature
3. Predation (Biology) — Juvenile literature
I.Title
591.7'34

ISBN 1 842 34003 4

Design: Richard Rowan
Artwork: Malcolm Porter
Consultant: Sue Fogden

Printed in Hong Kong by Wing King
Tong Co. Ltd

Acknowledgements
Photographs: *All by courtesy of Michael & Patricia
Fogden with the following exceptions: BBC Natural
History Unit* 14 top, 16/17 bottom, 22, 22/23 top, 23
bottom, 24 bottom, 26/27 bottom, 27 right, 28/29, 29

✸ CONTENTS ✸

❂ Predators and Prey ❂

Rainforests grow in warm, wet regions near the equator. They contain a greater variety of plants and animals than anywhere else on earth. The animals that live in the forests, like all animals, depend on plants for their food, although they do not all get it directly from plants.

Forest Food Chains

The eagle that swoops down and snatches a monkey from the tree-tops is a meateater, a carnivore. But the meat that it eats, the flesh of the monkey, is created from the plants that the monkey has eaten. Plant > monkey > eagle is an example of a food chain. All animals belong to one or more food chains. Some food chains have four or five links, but they all

Ambush

SITTING motionless with its front legs folded up under its head, this mantis looks more like a withered flower than a hungry killer. It goes unnoticed by other insects, but it is alert and waiting to pounce. When another insect comes within range, the mantis shoots out its spiky front legs and its victim is hopelessly trapped.

Gladiator spiders also ambush their prey, using an unusual kind of web. They hide, often close to

the ground, and wait for insects to pass below them. The gladiator spider (right) holds a small but stretchy net between its four front legs. When prey comes within range, the spider spreads its legs to expand the net and then drops it over the victim.

start with plants. Plants are eaten by herbivores (planteaters) and by omnivores (animals that eat plants and meat).

CHASING AND TRAPPING

Animals that catch and eat other creatures are called predators; the animals they catch are their prey.

Predators have two main ways of catching food: either they chase it or they lie in wait for it and take it by surprise. Spiders and a few other animals make traps to catch their prey.

Most of the predators in the rainforest are hunters. They usually see, smell or hear their prey from some distance away, and then go after it. The approach might be slow and stealthy, like that of the chameleon, or it might be a short, high-speed chase like that of an eagle weaving through the trees after a monkey. More often, it is a combination of the two. Cats and many snakes, for example, approach stealthily at first and then make a final high-speed strike.

◀ Silence and concentration are the predator's tools, followed by speed and strength. At the right moment, this jaguar will run down its victim.

⚙ INSECTS AND INSECT-EATERS ⚙

T HE MOST numerous creatures in the
rainforests are invertebrates: insects and
spiders and other small creatures. Many of
them, like butterflies and moths, are
planteaters. Many others, including
cockroaches, live as scavengers, eating dead
leaves and other debris on the forest floor.
Some are meateaters. But all are food for
larger creatures, including birds, amphibians,
reptiles and mammals.

Ants are everywhere on the ground and in
the trees. There are so many of them that
they probably weigh more than all the other
animals put together. More than 400
different kinds live in the Amazon forest of
South America. They feed on all kinds of
plant and animal matter and, in turn, are
eaten by many other animals.

ANTS ON THE MARCH

Army ants live in the tropics of Africa and
America. They live in enormous colonies,
some of which contain as many as 20 million
ants. Army ants feed mainly on other

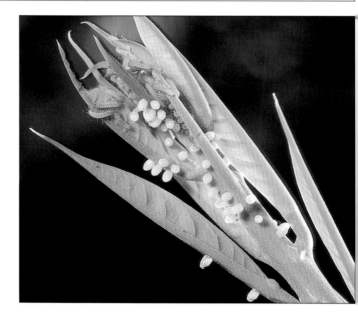

▲ Butterfly eggs and
caterpillars provide food for
huge numbers of birds and
other predators. Very few
caterpillars survive to grow
up into new butterflies.

▼ These army ants are
transporting a wasp larva
back to their nest. They bring
food home for the queen and
the thousands of workers
that look after her as she
lays her eggs.

6

▲ Termites have many enemies, but predators are often attacked by the large-jawed soldier termites when they break into the nests.

◀ Tree frogs eat huge numbers of insects in the rainforests.

▲ The white-plumed antbird perches close to columns of army ants and snaps up cockroaches and other insects as they scurry away from the ants.

insects, but no animal is safe from them. They will eat anything that cannot escape, including large snakes that have eaten big meals and cannot move quickly. Thousands of pairs of sharp jaws quickly reduce these animals to skeletons.

MAKING CAMP

Army ants have no permanent homes. If these huge colonies settled down in one place, they would soon run out of food. Instead, they 'camp' for a while, and then move on to new hunting grounds.

American army ants make their camps, or bivouacs, in sheltered spots, often between the buttress roots of large trees. Thousands of worker ants link their legs together to make a ball about a metre across. The queen and the thousands of other workers that tend her rest in this living tent at night. At daybreak the workers get restless and start to wander about. They gradually form into columns and march off to find food. Large individuals called soldiers march at the edges of the columns. The insects catch and kill anything in their path. They eat some of the food as they catch it, but store the rest by the sides of their paths and collect it on the return journey.

TERMITES

Termites are small, soft-bodied insects that live in large colonies. Many of them nest in trees or on the ground. Some termite species build enormous mounds that house several million insects. Termites are often mistaken for ants, although the two groups are not related. Ant-eating mammals usually eat lots of termites as well. They might actually prefer to eat termites because termites do not have stings and their soft bodies are easier to digest.

EATING ANTS

Although each ant is small, their nests or colonies may contain many thousands of individuals, and an animal can obtain a good meal by breaking into a nest. Some rainforest mammals are specialists in eating ants and termites, and eat little else. They usually have big claws to rip open the nests and long snouts to poke into them. Long sticky tongues help them lick up the ants efficiently.

GIANT ANTEATER

The giant anteater lives on the plains and in the forests of tropical America. It feeds mainly on large, ground-living ants. It finds the ants' nests with its excellent sense of smell. Its tongue is about

▲ A tamandua from the Amazon forest shows the long snout and large claws typical of most ant-eating mammals.

◀ Tamanduas are small tree-dwelling anteaters. They move slowly through the branches at night, clinging on with their tails as well as with their claws. They feed on termites as well as ants. This one is a northern tamandua from Central America.

▶ Clinging to a liana with its back legs and long furry tail, this silky anteater is ready to defend itself against eagles and other predators with its big front claws.

60 cm long and covered with thick saliva that traps the ants and prevents them from stinging its mouth. Anteaters have no teeth and they grind up their food with powerful stomach muscles.

An anteater probably needs to eat several thousand large ants every day, but it does not take them all from one nest. It visits many nests in turn and takes no more than a few hundred ants at a time. In this way it does not do too much damage to the colonies and can always be sure of food for another day.

SCALY ANTEATERS

Pangolins are called scaly anteaters because they are covered with tough, overlapping scales. Several species live in Africa and in Asia. All pangolins are excellent climbers. They use their large claws and the sharp edges of their scales to grip the tree trunks as they climb. And some of them can hang by their tails. The giant pangolin, which is about 150 cm long and weighs about 30 kg, lives on the ground and can eat many thousands of insects in one night. Thick mucus in its mouth and throat prevent it from being stung or bitten. A pangolin can roll itself into a scaly ball, and it is then safe from almost any large predator.

☸ FEATHERED PREDATORS ☸

THOUSANDS OF different kinds of insects and small creatures live in the rainforests and are food for hundreds of different birds. The birds' beaks are specially adapted for catching insects either on the ground, in the trees, or in the air.

Although there are not many small plants on the forest floor, there are always plenty of dead leaves and branches that have fallen from the canopy. There is also plenty of fallen fruit. These all provide food and shelter for worms, beetles, woodlice, slugs, snails, millipedes and other small scavenging animals. The scavengers are eaten by spiders, centipedes, carnivorous beetles and other small predators. All of these small creatures make the forest floor a great hunting ground for birds like pittas and antbirds.

ANTBIRDS AND PITTAS

About 250 species of antbirds live in South and Central America (although not all of them live in the

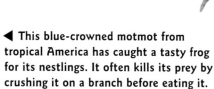

◀ This blue-crowned motmot from tropical America has caught a tasty frog for its nestlings. It often kills its prey by crushing it on a branch before eating it.

▶ The beady eyes of this scale-backed antbird are always on the lookout for ants and other juicy insects.

KINGFISHERS THAT DON'T FISH

KINGFISHERS do not all eat fish. Many members of this large family live and feed in the rainforests. The shovel-billed kingfisher lives in New Guinea. It has a massive beak like a shovel which it uses to dig for worms and other invertebrates in muddy ground. It also catches crabs in mangrove swamps. Paradise kingfishers also live in New Guinea and neighbouring areas. They perch on low branches and streak to the ground or to nearby leaves to catch lizards, worms or insects. The buff-breasted paradise kingfisher (left) lives in northern Australia.

◀ Trogons spend a lot of their time just sitting on leafy branches from which they streak out with their beaks wide open to scoop up insects in mid-air. This orange-bellied trogon lives in the rainforests of Central America.

forests). They are rather dumpy birds with fairly long legs, and nearly all of them live on or close to the ground. Their short, rounded wings are ideal for flying through dense vegetation, although they are not strong fliers. Large flocks, often containing several different species, move over the forest floor as they search for ants and other small creatures.

Pittas are small, colourful birds with short stubby tails. About 30 species live and feed on the rainforest floor. Apart from the African pitta they all live in Southeast Asia and on islands in the South Pacific. Most of them fly very little. Instead they run around scratching in the leaf litter for worms and insects, especially termites.

▶ Knee-deep in rotted leaf litter, this giant pitta is stuffed to bursting point with big fat ants.

WELL-NAMED WOODPECKER

Woodpeckers find their food by pecking into tree trunks and dragging out insects that feed there. Their beaks are long and sharp and the birds can hammer them into the trees as fast as twenty times a second. Woodpeckers also have long tongues that they push deep into the holes to drag out the insects. Specially formed feet, with two toes pointing forward and two pointing back, enable the birds to cling firmly to the trunks while they are hammering.

SUNBITTERNS AND POTOOS

The sunbittern lives in tropical America, usually near water. As well as snapping up insects and spiders among the decaying leaves, it catches frogs and crustaceans by jabbing its beak into pools of water. The bird is about 50 cm long, but difficult to see when resting on the ground. If it is disturbed, however, it spreads its wings in a spectacular display. Large eye-like markings appear on a golden background and would probably frighten most predators.

The potoo is even more difficult to find. It flies at night and catches moths and other large insects on the wing. During the day it sits motionless and looks just like a broken branch.

▼ When threatened the sunbittern spreads its wings in a frightening display.

▲ A black-cheeked woodpecker returns to its nest hole with some grubs that it has pecked from a tree trunk.

▲ Is it a bird or is it a branch? The potoo (above) sleeps like a log and keeps so still that other animals pass it by.

▲ The boat-billed heron (above right) lives close to rivers in the American rainforests. It comes out to hunt as the sun goes down and scoops up fish in its huge bill.

A NOSE FOR FOOD

Most vultures live in open country, using their amazing eyesight to spot dead and dying animals on the ground far below them. The king vulture of the American tropics is one of the few carrion-eating birds living in the forests. Unlike most other birds, it has a good sense of smell. It is not easy for birds to see carrion on the forest floor while they are flying in or above the canopy, so they need to be able to smell it. As well as eating dead birds and mammals, the king vulture feeds on fish stranded on the banks of rivers and lakes when flood waters subside.

The pauraque lives in Central America and hunts at night. It is almost invisible when sitting in the leaf litter by day.

▶ The king vulture's beak is not strong enough to rip fresh flesh. It is happier with decayed flesh. The frill of skin on its bill is called a wattle.

✸ Cold-Blooded Killers ✸

SNAKES, LIZARDS and crocodiles are reptiles. Many different kinds slither or scuttle through the rainforests. Many of them even climb trees. Reptiles are often described as cold-blooded animals, but they are not always cold. Their bodies stay at more or less the same temperature as their surroundings. In cold weather they cool down and become very slow, but in warm weather they can actually get quite hot, and then they can move very quickly.

When lying in wait for food, being able to hide is useful. Most rainforest snakes and lizards have skin that blends in with the vegetation or the forest floor. Certain lizards, particularly chameleons, can change their skin colour to match their backgrounds. They can wait and watch without being seen by their prey.

Boa's Tight Squeeze

Rainforests are home to the world's biggest snakes. The anaconda from South America reaches lengths of about 10 metres, although most specimens are a good deal smaller. The anaconda belongs to a group of snakes known as boas.

ANACONDA

The anaconda is rarely found far from rivers and spends much of the daytime basking in the shallows. It feeds mainly at night but it is too heavy to chase things, so it usually lies in wait on the river bank. Its prey includes fishes, birds, mammals and even crocodiles and caimans. Mammals are usually caught when they come to the river banks to drink.

The anaconda is not a poisonous snake. It either suffocates its victims by wrapping its huge body around them or it drags them into the water and drowns them. It easily overcomes tapirs and capybaras – pig-sized relatives of the guinea pigs – and then swallows them whole. This specimen is a female more than four metres long.

▲ This scrub python from the rainforest of northern Australia is not at all easy to spot among the dead leaves on the forest floor. It can slither quietly up to its prey without being seen.

Several other boas, including the boa constrictor, live in South America. The boa constrictor feeds on birds and mammals, which it catches and kills in the same way as the anaconda (see panel).

The emerald tree boa lives mainly in the trees, where it drapes itself over a branch and waits, beautifully camouflaged, until birds or monkeys come within range. Then it strikes rapidly, grabbing the prey in its mouth while hanging on with its tail. Although most tree-dwelling snakes detect their prey by sight, the tree boa's mouth is surrounded by heat-detectors that tell it when a warm-blooded animal approaches.

◀ A boa constrictor drapes its powerful coils over a buttress root. Boas live for months without food and sleep for days after a big meal. They can kill and swallow animals much larger than their heads.

▶ The emerald tree boa from tropical America wraps itself around a branch and waits for prey to arrive. It keeps its head uncovered so that heat-detectors around its mouth can tell when its prey is approaching.

LIZARDS IN THE TREES

Hundreds of different kinds of lizards live in rainforest trees, which they climb with the aid of sharp claws. Some of them can even glide from tree to tree. The big iguanas of the American rainforests feed mainly on flowers and fruits, but most lizards are predators. Their prey ranges from insects to deer and other mammals and is detected by sight and smell. Most lizards continually flick out their tongues to pick up scent particles from the surroundings.

CAREFUL CHAMELEONS

Chameleons move so slowly through the rainforest trees that it is hard to believe that they can catch insects. They rarely move more than one leg at a time. Each foot has toes that grip the branches like a pair of tongs and the chameleon makes sure that it has a good grip before moving another leg. The animals can also grip the branches with their tails, something that no other lizards can do.

Chameleons have unusual eyes, but excellent eyesight. Each eye sits in a turret that can swivel in all directions, allowing the lizard to look backwards with one eye and forwards with the other. When it spots an insect, the chameleon moves slowly towards it. Both eyes turn to focus on the prey and then the chameleon shoots out its tongue at lightning speed. The tongue is elastic and it can stretch to twice the length of the body. The prey is caught on the sticky tip of the tongue and pulled into the mouth.

▼ The green anole lizard blends beautifully with the forest leaves and is hidden from predators as well as from its prey. It lives in tropical America.

▲ This spiky lizard is called a forest dragon. It looks fierce, but it is really quite harmless to people. It feeds on insects and other small animals and its spiky appearance probably frightens its enemies.

▼ You have to be quick to catch a fly. The chameleon completes the operation in under a tenth of a second.

CLINGING GECKOES AND ANOLES

Geckoes are famous for their ability to walk upside down. The undersides of their broad toes are clothed with tiny branched hairs whose tips act like microscopic suction cups that can cling to almost any surface – including shiny wet leaves. Geckoes are mostly nocturnal and they feed mainly on insects, which they find by sight rather than by scent. They do not flick out their tongues like other lizards.

Unlike most lizards, geckoes have voices. The tokay gecko of Southeast Asia is up to 36cm long and is a rather noisy animal. When it is angry or alarmed, it opens its big mouth and yaps like a dog.

Anoles are fairly small lizards, most of which live in trees. Like geckoes, they have suction pads on their toes that enable them to cling to smooth surfaces. Anoles are omnivorous creatures, feeding partly on fruit and partly on insects. Most can change their colours to some extent, though not as quickly as chameleons. Over 150 kinds of anoles live in the warmer parts of America.

▲ Flying frogs live in the rainforests of Southeast Asia. Each of their large webbed feet acts like a little parachute, enabling them to glide up to 15 metres.

FLYING LIZARDS

Flying dragons live in the rainforests of Southeast Asia. They catch and eat insects on tree trunks and branches. Although they cannot really fly, they can glide as far as 20 metres from tree to tree. Their 'wings' are colourful flaps of skin supported by extra-long ribs. In the air they are bright enough to be mistaken for birds or butterflies, but as soon as they land on a tree trunk they fold their wings away and melt into the background. This helps them catch their food and avoid becoming food for other creatures.

▼ This gecko shows the broad toes typical of this group of lizards. Its large eyes help it to find insects at night.

▶ In full flight, this flying dragon clearly shows the delicate ribs that support its colourful wing flaps.

FROGS WITH BIG APPETITES

FROGS belong to the group of animals called amphibians. They resemble reptiles in being cold-blooded, but do not have scaly skins. Hundreds of different kinds live in the rainforests, either on the ground or in the trees. They feed on all sorts of insects, and some of them have such enormous mouths that they can swallow mice and other frogs. They often use their front feet to push their prey into their mouths. Large meals have to be helped on their way down the frog's throat, and the frog does this by pushing with its eyeballs! This horned frog comes from the South American rainforest. It is swallowing a lizard.

The parachute gecko has a loose fold of skin on both sides of its body, and this opens up to form a sort of parachute when the animal stretches its legs. It also has webbed feet and a flap all round its tail, and these all help to keep it airborne. The parachute gecko is not as good a glider as the flying dragon, but if it misses its target, it simply drifts to the ground and then climbs up another tree.

RUNNING ON WATER

Basilisk lizards live in dense waterside vegetation in the forests of tropical America. They drop into the water when alarmed by a predator and can actually run across the water surface on their long back legs. As long as they move quickly, their long fringed toes keep them up. If they slow down they sink into the water and then have to swim. They can also rear up on their back legs and run across the ground. Basilisks eat a mixture of plant and insect food and are eaten by large birds and caimans.

✸ DANGER IN THE WATER ✸

THE RIVERS THAT wind through the rainforests may look cool and welcoming but they are full of dangerous creatures. When the rivers are in flood, many of these creatures swim among the trees and snatch land animals that are unable to escape the rising waters. Predatory animals are also common in the mangrove swamps that grow along many tropical coasts.

Archer fishes live in the mangrove swamps of Southeast Asia and northern Australia. Although they catch most of their food in the water, they have a wonderful way of catching extra food when they are hungry. They shoot insects from overhanging plants by firing 'bullets' of water from their mouths.

CAIMANS AND CROCODILES

Caimans are reptiles belonging to the same family as crocodiles and alligators. They live in South America and spend a lot of time sunbathing on muddy banks, often in large numbers. They hunt mainly by sight, catching their prey either in the water or on land. For such large animals they are surprisingly agile and fast. They swim close to the banks and often catch mammals that have come down to drink. They tackle animals as big as pigs, usually dragging

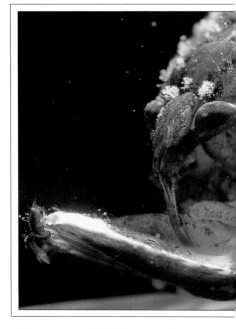

▲ In a savage fight for survival, a water bug attacks another water bug of its own kind.

▼ The dense vegetation (below left) typical of the rainforest edge is mirrored in this quiet lake, but lurking underneath the surface there may be many fierce and hungry predators.

▲ Piranhas may be fierce but their sharp teeth are no problem for a caiman (above right). This South American black caiman has just caught a large one.

▼ The eye-lash viper is a venomous snake that hunts close to the water. It feeds mainly on birds, which it catches when they come to drink.

them into the water before eating them. They also eat fishes, frogs, turtles and birds. Caimans themselves may be eaten by jaguars and also by large snakes.

Crocodiles also live in rainforest rivers. They behave just like caimans but, unlike caimans, they do not have bony plates on their bellies.

WHAT A SHOCK!

The electric eel lives in South America. It is up to three metres long and its body contains special muscles that generate electricity. These muscles, which account for up to half of the fish's weight, also store electricity like batteries. The fish electrocutes its prey by firing electric currents into the water. It feeds mainly on other fishes and frogs, but it actually generates enough electricity to kill a horse standing in the water. The fish usually lives in stagnant backwaters that do not contain much oxygen, but it makes up for this by periodically gulping air at the surface.

RAZOR TEETH

About 20 species of piranha fish live in the rivers of South and Central America. They feed mainly on other fish, but they are ferocious creatures and will attack almost any animal that enters the water. Although each fish is no more than about 60 cm long, they swim in large shoals. Their razor-sharp teeth carve slices of flesh from their victims and a shoal can reduce a large animal to a skeleton in a few minutes. Piranhas hunt mainly by scent and get excited when they smell blood in the water. Wounded animals are almost certain to be attacked.

MOST OF THE planteating animals of the rainforest live in the canopy, because that is where most of the food is. This means that most of the predators also have to live in the canopy, or at least go up there to feed. These tree-top hunters are all fairly small and generally very agile. Most of the carnivorous mammals living there are nocturnal, with large, forward-looking eyes that help them find their food and judge distances when leaping from branch to branch.

A variety of small cats, some no bigger than our pet cats, live in the rainforests. Several have been hunted so much for their beautiful fur that they are threatened with extinction.

BIG EYES AND SHARP EARS

Most forest cats hunt at night, but even those that hunt in the daytime need big eyes to spot their prey in the gloomy forest. They also have excellent hearing and a good sense of smell, although smell is much less important than sight and hearing when it comes to finding food. When they have spotted their prey, the cats slink quietly and slowly towards it and then pounce on it when they get near enough. They eat almost anything they can catch, but birds and small mammals, including monkeys, make up most of their food.

▶ Margays hunt mainly by day and are agile enough to catch monkeys and birds in the forest canopy. They can climb head-first down a tree trunk almost as easily as they can climb up.

▲ Ocelots are good climbers. They catch a lot of birds and, unlike other cats, remove most of the feathers before eating the flesh. So many ocelots have been killed for their fur that they have become quite rare.

◀ Clouded leopards are shy creatures and rarely seen. They climb well and can even crawl upside down along branches to reach their prey. Birds and monkeys are swatted with one of its large paws, but it often kills deer and wild pigs by dropping on to them from a branch.

▶ Fishing cats live in mangrove swamps and other wet forests. They catch some fish but probably exist mainly on frogs, crabs, insects and occasional birds.

LINSANGS AND GENETS

No small cats regularly hunt in the African rainforests. Their place is taken by linsangs and genets and other members of the mongoose family. The African linsang looks like a slender cat. It can run along the slimmest branches and seems to flow through the canopy as it searches for food. Genets are just as graceful. Both groups are nocturnal and rarely come down from the trees. Lizards, birds and their eggs and nestlings, and small mammals are their main prey.

NOSY COATIS

The ringtail coati, sometimes called the coatimundi, is a member of the racoon family. It lives in the forests of South America and is always sticking its long nose into things. Although it is a good climber, it finds most of its food by rooting around in debris on the forest floor. It sometimes eats lizards and mice, but beetles, ants, spiders,

▲ A white-nosed coati raids a banana tree. Coatis live mainly on meat but also enjoy fruit.

and other invertebrate animals make up most of its diet, together with generous helpings of fruit, which it gathers up from the ground or picks fresh from the tree-tops.

BUSHBABIES AND LORISES

Bushbabies and lorises are distant cousins of the monkeys. They look like small monkeys and often live side by side with them in the forests of Africa and Asia. While the monkeys roam the forests by day, bushbabies and lorises come out only after dark. Big eyes help them to find their way at night and also help them catch their food, though the animals rely more on sounds and smells to locate their prey in the first instance. They eat insects and other small animals, together with lots of fruit and flowers.

Bushbabies are amazingly agile creatures and use their long, strong back legs to make enormous leaps from tree to tree. Their long, bushy tails help them to steer and to keep their balance. They are so quick that they can catch moths in flight. Clinging tightly to a branch with its back feet, the bushbaby shoots its arms out and catches the insects in its hands.

Lorises are extremely slow creatures with short tails and they cannot leap at all. They rarely take more than one foot off a branch at a time. They find their prey mainly by scent, and creep slowly up to it and grab it with their teeth or hands. Lorises happily eat foul-tasting millipedes and even caterpillars with stinging hairs – though they may rub off the hairs before swallowing the flesh.

LONG-TAILED TARSIERS

Tarsiers live on various islands in Indonesia and the Philippines. They look like small bushbabies, but they have slender tails and their back legs are nearly twice as long as the body. They are only distantly related to bushbabies. Huge eyes and big ears help tarsiers find their prey at night. They hunt in trees or on the ground and usually capture their prey by leaping on to it and pinning it down with their long fingers. Insects are their main prey, but tarsiers also eat lizards, birds and bats. They make enormous leaps from tree to tree, pushing off with their powerful back legs and judging the distances accurately with their big eyes. They use their long tails as rudders.

▲ Tarsiers can leap long distances between trees. They use their tails as rudders. From a lookout post in a tree, they survey the area for likely prey.

◀ As well as good sight, bushbabies have sensitive noses that can pick up the scent of desirable food in the still air of the forest.

● MIGHTY HUNTERS ●

MOST OF THE animals that live in the rainforest are preyed upon by other animals higher up the food chains. Big cats and eagles are at the top of the food chains. They are less numerous than smaller animals but are so strong and fierce that they have no natural enemies. Only humans hunt them.

GREAT CATS

Three of the world's big cats live in rainforests, although they live in other habitats as well. Jaguars live in America, tigers in Asia, and leopards in Africa and Asia. All of these cats are solitary animals that live by themselves. They usually stalk their prey slowly for a while and then cover the last few metres with a sprint or with one mighty leap. Leopards and jaguars sometimes simply lie on a branch and drop on to any animal that walks underneath. They kill by biting their prey in the neck

JAGUARS AND LEOPARDS

Cats are mostly good climbers and spend a lot of time in the trees. Their coats provide excellent camouflage among the sun-dappled leaves. Jaguars are most common in dense forests. They catch monkeys, sloths and birds in the trees, but most of their hunting is done on the ground, where they catch deer, peccaries and capybaras. Peccaries are pig-like creatures, while the capybara is like an enormous guinea-pig. Leopards eat many kinds of animals, including antelopes, monkeys and pigs.

▶ Leopards are usually pale with black spots like the jaguar, but in the wettest forests many of them are sooty black and their spots are hardly visible. These leopards are often called panthers or black panthers.

▼ Well camouflaged by its spotted coat, the jaguar watches intently while waiting for the right moment to attack.

TIGERS

Rainforest tigers tend to be smaller and darker than other tigers. Their stripes conceal them well in the dense vegetation that grows along the river banks where they hunt. Tigers rarely ambush their victims. They go in search of food when they are hungry, stalking their prey slowly until they are within about 20 metres and then charging rapidly. The prey is often knocked down with one blow from a huge paw. Tigers will eat any animal that they can catch, but deer, antelopes and pigs are their main prey. They also kill and eat water buffalo and sometimes take elephant calves.

▶ Tigers are good swimmers and frequently plunge into rivers to catch water creatures.

EAGLES IN THE TREE-TOPS

The world's biggest eagles live in the rainforests. They are the main predators in the canopy and are at the top of all the food chains there. Eagles' wings are very broad, but quite short for such large birds, and they also have long rudder-like tails. This gives the birds great agility, enabling them to chase their prey between the trunks and branches at high speed. They catch monkeys and many other animals with their huge talons, and tear them to pieces with their hooked beaks. The birds have excellent eyesight to spot their prey, sometimes from a high perch in one of the emergent trees that stand high above the canopy or else while soaring or gliding over it.

CROWNED HEAD

Crowned eagles are named for the crest, or crown, of feathers at the back of the head. They live in Africa, mainly in forests but also in more open country. They kill forest antelopes on the ground as well as

▼ This white-throated capuchin monkey, reaching for water in a tree hole, must always be on the look-out for harpy eagles ready to scoop it up in their talons.

▲ The crowned eagle, with its crown folded down, is alert for any movement that might indicate a meal.

monkeys in the tree-tops. The eagles weigh about 4 kg and their prey is often as big or even bigger. Prey that is too heavy to be carried is cut up and parts of it are hidden in the trees for another time.

BIGGEST EAGLE

The harpy eagle is the biggest of all eagles. Up to 110 cm long and weighing up to 8 kg, it feeds mainly on monkeys and sloths, and even tackles spiny porcupines. Its talons are as big as a man's hands and it can plunge into the canopy to snatch its prey at a speed of 80 km/h. It lives in tropical America. The New Guinea harpy eagle hunts in or below the forest canopy. This very rare bird usually sits on a branch and streaks out to chase other birds. It also plunges to the ground to catch young pigs and other mammals. A good runner, it even chases its prey on the ground.

▼ Also known as the monkey-eating eagle, the Philippine eagle is one of the rarest birds of prey. It is almost as big as the harpy eagle and, as well as catching monkeys, it sometimes drops down to snatch small deer from the forest floor.

❋ GLOSSARY ❋

Amazon The great river in South America and the area around it, which contains the world's largest rainforest.

Ambush A method of capturing prey by lying in wait, usually well hidden, and pouncing when the prey comes within reach.

Amphibian Any member of the group of backboned animals that includes frogs, toads and newts. Most of them grow up in water and live on land when they mature. The name means 'double life'.

Buttress roots Large roots that spread from the base of a tree like low walls and help to support the trunk.

Camouflage Skin colours and patterns that help an animal blend with its surroundings and avoid the attention of predators.

Canopy The 'roof' of the rainforest, formed by the leafy branches of the trees. It is usually about 30 metres above the ground and it cuts off most of the light from the forest floor.

Carnivore An animal that feeds mainly on meat, or flesh.

Carrion Dead meat.

Cold-blooded A cold-blooded animal is one that cannot maintain its body at a constant temperature. Reptiles and amphibians are cold-blooded. Their body temperatures are usually similar to those of the surroundings, so they are not necessarily cold. In tropical forests, cold-blooded animals can actually be very hot.

Constrictor The name given to any snake that kills by wrapping its body around its prey and squeezing it until it cannot breathe.

Emergent Any large tree that grows above the rainforest canopy.

Extinction The total disappearance of a particular plant or animal species from the earth, often brought about when people destroy forests and other habitats and leave the animals nowhere to live. Many rainforest species are in danger of extinction.

Food chain A sequence of plants and animals that feed on each other and pass energy along the

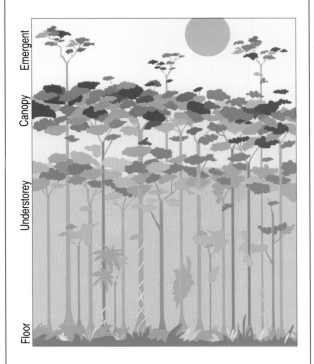

▲ A rainforest has layers of vegetation: low shrubs on the forest floor, slender young trees that form an understorey below the vast, dense canopy of tree-tops. At intervals taller trees called emergents poke their heads through the canopy. All the plants are trying to get a share of the sunlight.

chain. An example is flower – fly – spider – bird – cat. There are rarely more than five links in a chain and each one starts with a plant. Food chains in a particular habitat are all linked together into a complex food web.

Habitat The natural home of a plant or animal species. It may be a whole forest or just a tree trunk, or even a pool of water trapped by a plant.

Herbivore An animal that feeds on plants.

Invertebrate Any animal without a backbone, including insects, worms and spiders.

Larva (plural larvae) Stage in the development of some animals. Caterpillars and tadpoles are larvae.

Leaf litter The layer of dead and decaying leaves on the forest floor.

Mammal Any member of the class of animals in which the females feed their babies with milk. Mammals are warm-blooded and most of them have hair or fur. Examples include monkeys, deer, cats and elephants.

Mangrove swamp A coastal swamp covered with

ENDANGERED!

RAINFORESTS are vitally important to the well-being of the world but they are in danger of destruction. Many of the animals and plants featured in this book are under threat from forest clearance. If you are interested in knowing more about rainforests and in helping to conserve them, you may find these addresses and websites useful.

Friends of the Earth, Rainforest Campaign, 26-28 Underwood Street, London N1 7JQ

Rainforest Foundation, A5 City Cloisters, 188-96 Old St, London EC1V 9FR

Worldwide Fund for Nature
WWF (Australia), Level 5, 725 George Street, Sydney, NSW 2000
WWF (South Africa), 116 Dorp Street, Stellenbosch 7600
WWF (UK), Panda House, Weyside Park, Cattershall Lane, Godalming, Surrey GU17 1XR

Worldwide Fund for Nature
http://www.wwf-uk.org

Friends of the Earth
http://www.foe.co.uk

Environmental Education Network
http://envirolink.org.enviroed/

Rainforest Foundation
http://rainforestfoundationuk.org

Rainforest Preservation Foundation
http://www.flash.net/~rpf/

Survival International
http://www.survival.org.uk

Sustainable Development
http://iisd1.iisd.ca/

Rainforest Action Network
http://www.igc.apc.org/ran/intro.html

◀ The map shows the location of the world's main rainforest areas.

NORTH AMERICA
EUROPE
ASIA
Tropic of Cancer
AFRICA
Equator
Tropic of Capricorn
SOUTH AMERICA
AUSTRALIA

evergreen trees whose stilt-like roots form dense tangles.

Nocturnal Active by night.

Omnivore An animal that eats both plant and animal matter.

Oxygen A gas in the air and in water that enables animals to breathe.

Predator Any animal that hunts and kills other animals for food.

Prey Any animal that is killed by another for food.

Queen The name given to the egg-laying female in a colony of social insects, such as ants or termites.

Reptile Any member of the group of backboned animals that includes tortoises, crocodiles, snakes and lizards. They have scaly skins.

Saliva The juice in the mouth of an animal that lubricates food and begins the process of digestion.

Scavenger An animal that feeds mainly on dead and decaying matter.

Talon A sharp claw, especially of a bird of prey.

Top predator Any predator at the top of a food chain. The tiger is a good example. It has no predators.

Tropical Describes the tropics – the warm areas around the equator.

Understorey The layer of vegetation growing below the canopy, consisting mainly of young trees.

Venomous Having venom or poison that can be fired at or injected into another animal. The venom is used for defence or to kill prey.

Warm-blooded Warm-blooded animals keep their bodies at a constant high temperature, no matter what the surrounding temperature may be. Birds and mammals are warm-blooded animals.

❋ INDEX ❋